FITTING IN

for Square Pegs in the Round Holes of Life

By Pat Getter

www.patgetter.com

Fitting In

Pat Getter

FITTING IN

*for Square Pegs
in the Round Holes of Life*

(c) 2014, Pat Getter, All Rights Reserved

This publication may not be reproduced, stored in a retrieval system or transmitted in whole or in part, in any form or by any means, electronic, mechanical, photocopying, recording or otherwise without the prior written permission of the publisher or the author.

First Published July 2013

ISBN-13: 978-0615846309
ISBN-10: 0615846300

Premiere Projects
eBook Publishing & Promotions

Premiere Projects
Las Vegas, NV 89118
www.PremiereProjects.com

Fitting In

TABLE OF CONTENTS

ABOUT THE AUTHOR 7
WHO ARE YOU? 9
DO YOU CARE? 11
BEGGARS CAN'T BE CHOOSERS 13
EMOTIONAL SATISFACTION WON'T LAST 15
WE ARE ALL REPLACEABLE 17
TAKE WORK SERIOUSLY, NOT YOURSELF.......19
WHO WAS I? WHO AM I?.......................................21
DEADWOOD DOESN'T FLOAT...............................27
THREE CAN KEEP A SECRET 31
KEEP YOUR EYE ON THE PRIZE..........................35
TELL THE EMPEROR HE'S NAKED 37
HAVE A VOICE, EARN A VOTE............................39
NEVER ASSUME ANYTHING 41
WHEN IT'S NOT WRONG..43
DRESS FOR SUCCESS ... NAH!..............................45
WATCH YOUR LANGUAGE 47
JUNK YARD DOG, NOT PIT BULL 49
MAINTAIN INDIVIDUAL DIVERSITY 51
A SINGULAR SENSATION 55
ENJOY YOUR 15 MINUTES.....................................59
DID YOU FIND IT?..61

Fitting In

ABOUT THE AUTHOR

Pat Getter decided when she was in seventh grade that she wanted to be a journalist. Her first big break was interviewing the junior high school custodian – and she's had an interesting career ever since.

Pat wrote for her high school and college newspapers, then after getting her Master of Journalism at UCLA decided to concentrate on television news. After nearly a decade of on-camera anchoring and reporting, Pat put her reporting skills, judgment and experience to work in corporate America, specializing in media relations and handling many significant events. She was interviewed by the Wall Street Journal and appeared on NBC's "Today" show among hundreds of national and international media and trade press while serving as the corporate worldwide media spokesperson for a multibillion-dollar product recall that involved more than 600 lawsuits. Even after she left the company, she was deposed three times.

Based on that experience, Pat has authored "Deposition vs. Root Canal: Preparation Techniques to Make Dental Work the *Only* Painful Experience" available in paperback and e-book formats.

In Houston, Pat established her own PR firm before she and her husband transferred to Washington, D.C., and she became vice president of communications for a major trade association.

Fitting In

After several years and seeking a change of pace, she moved to Las Vegas and was the public relations manager for a famous Strip hotel and casino.

Pat then returned to television, where she wrote, produced and hosted a number of programs connecting citizens to their government through Clark County TV.

Now Pat focuses her skills speaking about grammar, customer relations and fitting in. From years of being an accomplished writer and proofreader, Pat offers compelling and humorous insights into "The Trouble with 'Typoes,' Grammar Goofs and Sloppy Spelling: Mistakes Can Cost Millions or Muddy Your Message." From her years of being an accomplished consumer, she offers an entertaining and relevant look at "Customer Relation Experiences: Do YOU Top Santa Claus?" And from her years of being in bad jobs at good times and good jobs at bad times, she speaks about "Fitting In: for Square Pegs in the Round Holes of Life."

In her spare time, Pat is president of Doberman Rescue of Nevada, a non-profit organization dedicated to rehoming this noble breed into the forever homes they richly deserve.

To contact Pat:
6380 Golden Goose Lane
Las Vegas, NV 89118
702-467-5217
www.patgetter.com ☆ pat@patgetter.com

WHO ARE YOU?

Who are you?

That's the pressing question The Who asks in their iconic rock music classic and which the TV show "CSI: Crime Scene Investigation" uses as its theme every week.

It's a simple enough question – but only if you have the answer!

If you're not sure, then I suggest you start with a fundamental philosophy so eloquently articulated and immortalized by that iconic comic strip and TV cartoon character Popeye the sailor man:

I YAM WHAT I YAM.

Just to be crystal clear, I am not talking about those orange potato-looking vegetables you slather at Thanksgiving with marshmallows and brown sugar.

I'm talking about your integrity and individualism.

You.

Yourself.

A Singular Sensation.

Don't ever lose, sacrifice or compromise them. Don't hide, marginalize or forget them.

There may be times you will have to finesse, strategize or leverage them.

But learn how and when.

Fitting In

DO YOU CARE?

Haven't we all found ourselves in situations and circumstances that we're not crazy about? Maybe you love your job but some of your co-workers, well, not so much. Or you have great work colleagues, but the work hours and the travel time, well, not so much!

Or maybe everything about your work is great, but you belong to a car club, a bowling league or even a church group and you're not feeling the love.

Or maybe it's just one individual: your mother-in-law, perhaps? The boss's spouse? Your BFF's significant other? For whatever reason, in these groups or around that one person, you don't make a connection or you feel out of place.

But here's the fundamental question: do you care? Do you even care if you feel like a square peg in the round hole? I admit that I do, so let's do this: Think back as far as you can. Was there ever a time – even once – when you thought to yourself, I hope this person or these people like me or can accept me for who I am.

If your answer is yes, then you do care about fitting in and therefore you do care about feeling like the square peg in the round hole of life.

Fitting In

So then, what do you do? I've learned that we have to figure out how best to navigate the perils of just being ourselves! After all, I YAM WHAT I YAM!

There ARE things that we can control and that's a good place to start.

So let's look at what they are in the wacky world of work.

BEGGARS CAN'T BE CHOOSERS

If the moon were in the seventh house and Jupiter aligned with Mars, we would all get to choose where we would work and we would have perfect jobs. But, let's face it – there are only so many openings in a chocolate factory – or a liquor store!

For many of the rest of us, we wind up working jobs with factors or conditions we don't especially like such as the number of hours per day, the shift or the location. When gasoline prices are high, a great job that is 40 miles away suddenly is not as desirable. We have to weigh all those factors against the salary and benefits and decide if the position is worth it.

Fundamentally, it is the nature of the work itself and the people with whom we have to work that eventually get to us in the workplace and become the make-it-or-break-it. And in a tough economy, sometimes you just have to bite the bullet on these two factors when beggars can't be choosers.

Nobody takes a lot of comfort in "be glad you have a job" when the job sucks and the people suck even more, but there is truth in knowing it could be worse. Try to hang onto that thought – at least until you have another job and can give proper notice.

Fitting In

And let's discuss for a moment, what constitutes proper notice?

Pat Getter

EMOTIONAL SATISFACTION WON'T LAST

"I QUIT!"

We've all seen cartoons that depict some employee standing on his supervisor's desk either mooning his boss or wagging his finger as he shouts those words. And, I know I've envisioned how it would feel if and when I got the same opportunity to make such a grandstand. Have you?

But realistically, the business world is small and, as the saying goes, you don't want to burn your bridges. So most everyone who leaves a job does so in the conventional way: writes a dignified letter of resignation with a reasonable amount of notice and thanks the company for the opportunity to have served.

While mooning the boss gives you tremendous emotional satisfaction, it would be very short-lived and could be damaging long-term. And you really have to think about what is best for you down the road. Unless you don't intend to ever work again, having the story about mooning your boss follow you to every job interview does not help your chances of being hired somewhere else.

I was very lucky after I wrote my first resignation letter that it did NOT bite me in the butt. I suppose my employer wrote it off as being

Fitting In

from a young inexperienced reporter early in her career who would soon discover that all TV newsrooms are the same. I don't remember all of what I said but the phrase "jump off this sinking ship" sticks in my mind.

So think twice – three or four times, if necessary – before making any emotional outbursts. Even when not accompanied by standing on your supervisor's desk with your bare butt in the air, declarations of quitting or resigning or crying can become tedious if they are seen as manipulative tools to get your way.

The same goes for "not getting mad but getting even." There can be tremendous *momentary* satisfaction – but it is extremely dangerous and can easily backfire with long-lasting consequences.

You want to get even? Wait until you win the Powerball.

Pat Getter

WE ARE ALL REPLACEABLE

Look, we are all replaceable, but especially in a tight economy when so many others are looking for work, some of whom are willing to be underemployed. The moment you think you are irreplaceable you become imminently replaceable. Just ask any local market TV reporters or anchors who have gotten dollar signs in their eyes when renegotiating a contract.

I started my television career in Jacksonville, Fla., for $6,000 per year. And six grand was not much then either. I used to tell people I was paid in sunshine and all the oranges I could eat. Actually, Jacksonville was far enough north that there were few oranges, but they did have alligators – and a few sharks-in-training. And if I didn't take that TV job, they had thousands of budding journalists who would have given their left arm to have it.

The pay was so incredibly low that I had to offset my rent by helping out in the complex's laundry room one night a week handing out change. Here I was a local TV reporter and anchor handing out coins for the washing machines because I didn't make enough money to pay my rent and other bills. By day, interviewing Sam Donaldson; by night, flipping quarters and soap flakes. Yup, TV news is definitely glamorous!

Fitting In

Pat and Dusty interview Sam Donaldson for "News for Little People," 1973

From Jacksonville I worked in TV news in Oklahoma City and then Cincinnati. It was a news director there who revealed a valuable work insight: if you tell me that you're unhappy here or thinking about leaving, then I will begin looking for your replacement. You better hope I don't find your replacement before you find your next job.

In television news, the saying is, you are only as good as your last story. In business, the saying is, what will you do for me tomorrow?

Work for tomorrow to remain un-replaced.

TAKE WORK SERIOUSLY, NOT YOURSELF

Some people are too anal. Don't be one of them.

It's one thing to take your work seriously. It's something else to take yourself seriously.

Lighten up.

Work hard, be thorough and professional and get the job done. But there's no need to be uptight and overbearing.

Have a good laugh at your own expense, and a little self-deprecating humor goes a long way to break the ice with co-workers and bosses. That doesn't mean wear a water-spraying flower in your lapel – but it does mean having confidence in your ability to perform so that you can stay relaxed as you get the job done. Not only does it make people comfortable to be around you, a work environment without additional stress is definitely more productive.

Fitting In

WHO WAS I? WHO AM I?

I am one box away from a lampshade on my head. What about you?

I better explain.

For more than 35 years, I have either been in broadcast media or media relations. I've either conducted the interviews or been interviewed. My career has included positions in corporate America, a trade association, a county government, plus being a sole proprietor, a fancy way of saying I was my own company of one employee. I know corporate babblespeak and can write on flip charts and tape those giant sheets on walls of conference rooms with the best of them.

My venture into the corporate world was with a Fortune-100 company. I wound up with some very high profile – albeit not necessarily high paying or fast track – positions that I thoroughly enjoyed, but it was clear to me from the get-go that I was never going to be an insider there. I always thought I was a classic case of not fitting in.

This was a company of mostly scientists, engineers and technicians. Not to say that scientists, engineers and technicians can't be charming, engaging individuals, but the company culture had its creative boundaries outside of those disciplines. And what drove this home to me was when I was told to take the Wilson Learning Social Style Test.

These days, companies use other tests to determine if a potential employee is a good match for their particular corporate culture. And they usually do it before they hire you. But back then, this was the standard and it was administered after you were an employee.

There are four broad categories in the Wilson Learning Social Style test: analytical, driver, amiable and expressive. There are then four combinations of each style within each broad style. So, for example, within the driver category you could be an analytical-driver, amiable-driver, expressive-driver and driver-driver.

If you look at the chart for expressives, you can see I was an amiable-expressive, just one box short of expressive-expressive. And that's the person I would expect to see wearing a lampshade on her head! It doesn't get any more expressive than that!

For this discussion, it doesn't matter what the test questions were, only the results.

There was no stated category for jerk-jerk, but they were there, too.

How then, would I ever survive in a predominately analytical, driver, amiable environment?

ANALYTICAL-ANALYTICAL	DRIVER-ANALYTICAL	ANALYTICAL-DRIVER	DRIVER-DRIVER
ANALYTICAL		DRIVER	
AMIABLE-ANALYTICAL	EXPRESSIVE-ANALYTICAL	AMIABLE-DRIVER	EXPRESSIVE-DRIVER
ANALYTICAL-AMIABLE	DRIVER-AMIABLE	ANALYTICAL-EXPRESSIVE	DRIVER-EXPRESSIVE
AMIABLE		EXPRESSIVE	
AMIABLE-AMIABLE	EXPRESSIVE-AMIABLE	AMIABLE-EXPRESSIVE **ME**	EXPRESSIVE-EXPRESSIVE *WEARS LAMPSHADE ON HEAD?*

It helped that my job was one that few people were qualified to do and even fewer wanted to do. But your social style still has to do with how people *perceive* you. Interestingly, the test evaluation said it was "perfectly normal and okay" to be as you are. "There is no need, nor is it advisable for you to try to permanently change aspects of your behavior."

But then it said you may want to *"temporarily* modify your behavior to limit tension and help others to feel more comfortable with you."

Wait. Just. A. Minute.

Did you just tell me that people were tense and uncomfortable with me?

Do *you* ever feel that way?

Fitting In

It's knowing *when* and *how* to *temporarily* modify your behavior that's the key. Be in control and you won't need to compromise your integrity.

These "social style" and "versatility" learning tests are the epitome of profiling – personality profiling – which in the workplace is nearly as dangerous as anything racial or ethnic. When people try to fit your personality into previously defined categories, then they see and analyze all your future behavior through the rose-colored – or gray-colored glasses – the personality profile created.

As an amiable-expressive, the charts said I was a high-assertive and high-responsive person: emphasized ideas by tone change; expressions were aggressive, dominant, quick, clear or fast-paced; had a firm handshake; made statements rather than ask questions; let everyone know what I wanted, leaned forward to make a point; was animated; smiled, nodded, frowned; had frequent eye contact while listening; used friendly gestures; shared personal feelings; was attentive, responsive and enjoyed the relationship.

Your point?

And what happens when you've taken more than one personality test, which I did?

The Myers-Briggs Type Indicator is a well-known test that measures an individual's psychological type preferences. Supposedly if a company knows the strengths each of us brings to our work, it can reduce unproductive interpersonal and intra-organizational conflict and begin building working coalitions.

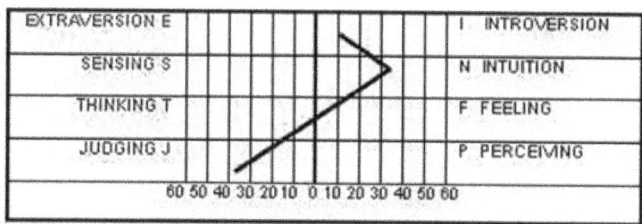

For those playing the home game, there are four scales and two opposite preferences on each scale making 16 possible combinations. According to MBTI, my Reported Type was INTJ – I for Introversion (opposite Extraversion), N for Intuition (opposite Sensing), T for Thinking (opposite Feeling) and J for Judging (opposite Perceiving). Got that?

On Myers-Briggs, I was an intuitive introvert: an original mind, great drive for my own ideas and purposes; a fine power to organize a job and carry it through with or without help; skeptical, critical, independent, determined and sometimes stubborn. I needed to learn to yield less important points in order to win the most important.

Alex, I'll take Psychobabble for $500.

Fitting In

Amiable-expressive. Intuitive-introvert.
Who was I? Who am I? Who are you?
I YAM WHAT I YAM.

If you try to be who or what the psychologists tell you they think you are and your employers expect you to be, you will feel as though your head will explode.

DEADWOOD DOESN'T FLOAT

I once had to report to a woman who became supervisor of the public relations group after being transferred from the finance department. What she knew about dealing with the media you could put on a sty on the eye of a gnat. She was the epitome of a large corporation not knowing what to do with someone who no longer was of any value. But rather than just letting her go, one department foisted her onto another, not caring that they were preserving a piece of deadwood. She was no longer *their* deadwood so she was no longer *their* problem.

If you're lucky, working for supervisors who have no clue will mean you have free rein either because they dare not admit to knowing less than you do or because they give you a chance to demonstrate your capabilities during their own steep learning curve. Hope springs eternal and maybe they even appreciate having a first lieutenant to count on?

Not gonna happen.

More than likely they will question everything you do because they will feel threatened by their own ignorance and the fear it creates, regularly challenging your work output and decisions just to feel involved and thinking that somehow that keeps you on your toes. We all know what it really does is irritate the snot out of you.

But, don't overreact. If there was ever a time to keep your head down, this is it. Do your work. Answer the questions. Be collegial. Smile. Doesn't mean you have to eat lunch together or go for a drink after work. You can ask if they had a nice weekend and not really care. It's just being polite. This, too, shall pass.

Just be certain not to give your supervisors ANY reasons to believe that you are being uncooperative or resistant to change. And, believe me, when you have to report to someone who knows substantially less about the job than you do – and it happens all the time – it is easy to get frustrated or angry about workplace inequities and injustices.

But this is not the time to stomp your feet and tell them off.

Why?

Let's think about this for a moment. Are you a student of television? Notice how on the classic ensemble dramas, the doctors, attorneys, FBI agents, CSI investigators and police are always berating each other, their adversaries and especially their supervisors and bosses all in the name of just blowing off steam? And then life goes on for another episode. And you know why this is acceptable? BECAUSE IT'S NOT REAL! Because only on television dramas and in movies can employees talk back, yell at and argue with their supervisors and bosses and get away with it. That's why they have that disclaimer in tiny print at the end that reads, "Any resemblance to real persons, either living or dead is a coincidence." In the real world you can be demoted, suspended or fired. Maybe not on the spot, but eventually.

So, whatever you do, don't talk about it.

Fitting In

THREE CAN KEEP A SECRET ...

I am the worst when it comes to gossip. Love to hear all about it. Love to spread it. I am nosier than an anteater.

But you may as well be playing with a blowtorch and a barrel of gasoline if you gossip in the workplace.

No matter how you couch your tidbit – this is just between you and me, promise you won't repeat this to anyone, I'll deny I ever said it – we are all human, we have our weaknesses, we believe we can pass gossip on to just that one other person who also promises not to repeat it to anyone, to keep it just between us and then before you know it, BAM, something you said gets back to just the person you didn't want to know or hear about it. And you're finished.

Benjamin Franklin had the perfect solution way back in 1735 – yeah, *1735* – when he wrote in Poor Richard's Almanac. Many still haven't learned this lesson: *Three may keep a secret if two of them are dead.*

We are more efficient now: *TWO MAY KEEP A SECRET IF ONE OF THEM IS DEAD.*

It doesn't get any plainer than that.

Fitting In

Ben Franklin authored the Almanac
using the alias of R. Saunders

But it is a very hard lesson to learn. And it can be learned hard. Especially if you love gossip.

Why is gossip so dangerous? Oh, let me count the ways. But first, let me define gossip. For this discussion, I use a very wide brush.

It's not just "did you hear that Marsha was dating Jack even though he just broke up with Marsha's best friend, Heather, and Heather doesn't even know yet about Marsha and Jack. Maybe

Marsha even caused the breakup – hmm, how about that?"

Gossip in this context includes what you think about your supervisor or other employees or any of their work product or anything about your own work product or about the company in general.

The danger, as the saying suggests, is who can you trust. The colleagues with whom you shared your frustrations and exasperations today because you thought they could be trusted not to repeat them may stab you in the back tomorrow. It might not be on purpose. But it doesn't matter. Because that bond of confidentiality weakens with each additional link until it's repeated without any proviso or disclaimer and at that point it's bound to get back to the wrong person.

And if it *is* on purpose, well, nothing personal, of course. Just all in a day's work.

And, as relationships go, your Best Friend Forever today could tomorrow be your WEE – Worst Enemy Ever. Or WWIT: What Was I Thinking?

So, sharing gossip, especially about work-related issues, is always risky.

You better calculate that risk very carefully before starting any sentence with "between you and me …"

Fitting In

Best advice: if you're one of the two people and you're the one still breathing, the only one hearing your frustrations should be your dearly departed great grandma.

Bottom line: if you work at a job that is not fulfilling or you work with people you really aren't crazy about, keep it to yourself and keep your eye on the prize.

KEEP YOUR EYE ON THE PRIZE

What is the prize? It's whatever goal you achieved by being there. Maybe taking that job paid for medical benefits you previously had to pay out of your own pocket or could not afford at all. Maybe the work schedule gave you a much needed opportunity to spend more time with your family. Or maybe you are getting valuable experience that one day will pay off with a better position, maybe even somewhere else.

Whatever the reason, don't lose sight of the tradeoff you made and the personal inner rewards you are reaping from it. Despite whatever outer difficulties the tradeoff created, those prizes are strong motivators when everything else stinks.

Fitting In

TELL THE EMPEROR HE'S NAKED

Remember the Hans Christian Andersen fairy tale about the emperor's new clothes? Turns out he wasn't wearing any but no one would tell him because the weavers had spun their story that only the stupid or incompetent could not see the threads.

The modern metaphor of telling the emperor he is naked means pushing back on bosses when you disagree with an idea or conclusion rather than just agreeing with them for the sake of sucking up and getting ahead. Many leaders are surrounded by "yes-men/women," but true leaders want people around them who will tell them the truth – not what they assume their bosses want to hear – and will not be intimidated by their position.

When important business decisions are at stake, admiring shiny threads of imaginary clothes is one transparency you don't want or need.

Fitting In

HAVE A VOICE, EARN A VOTE

Employees want to be heard. Whether it's through a suggestion box or face to face with the CEO, employees want a voice in what is going on around them.

But keep in mind that having a voice is not the same as having a vote. Bosses may listen to what you have to say but that doesn't mean that they will do what you ask.

Still, you owe it to yourself and to your employer to let your voice be heard. If for no other reason, your conscience will be clear that you did your due diligence.

And perhaps over time, with enough words of wisdom through that voice, you will earn the respect to be entitled to a vote.

Fitting In

NEVER ASSUME ANYTHING

There is an expression: Never assume; it just makes an ASS out of U and ME.

Truer words cannot be spoken.

I took an Italian class my first quarter as a freshman at UCLA and on the very first day I was smitten by a fellow student named Brian. We became buddies but Brian never asked me out. Several years later at a fraternity party, when I was so over Brian, he and I were talking and I just had to ask him why he had never asked me out. Surely he knew I was interested in him.

And this is what he said: *I was so afraid that I would fall head over heels in love I didn't dare jeopardize my athletic scholarship and my grades. So I didn't.*

Who knew? How could I have figured? In my wildest imagination THAT was never the reason. I ASSUMED it was because I wasn't pretty, skinny or tall enough or didn't belong to a sorority or maybe he preferred blondes and redheads.

This is a valuable lesson to learn. Think about how many times you start a sentence with "well, I assumed that …"

So don't.

Speculate all you want about some circumstance and use every ounce of deductive reasoning you can muster, but before you leap to any *conclusions* upon which you will take any action, make choices or implement decisions, go to the source and get the real answer.

You may have to wait awhile to find out but eventually you will find out.

It's been nearly 45 years since a high school chum accepted and then declined my invitation to go to the vice-versa dance. I saw him at a 40th reunion get-together but the timing wasn't right. Maybe I'll ask him at the 50th reunion.

Pat Getter

WHEN IT'S NOT WRONG

Among my many jobs was to produce a weekly company newsletter, which I did for four years. This was back in the day when I wrote all the copy, a photographer shot and developed pictures, a third employee typeset the copy and a graphic artist set the copy and photos in a layout, which I then edited and approved. The company had its own print shop, and we distributed several thousand copies for our local employees each week.

My boss had a philosophy – which I still embrace – about printed materials: *it's not wrong until it goes out wrong.*

That meant if you saw a mistake that somehow had been missed during proofing – even on newsletters or monthly magazines already printed and ready to be distributed – you would reprint it, all three thousand copies. If it didn't go out wrong, then it wasn't wrong. No matter the cost or time involved to redo it.

How many of us have such pride in our work product and care enough about our work ethic to go to such lengths? Email and text messages have just about killed spelling and proper grammar and that has taken its toll on printed materials and signage.

We see it all around us. "Rasberry," "seperate" and "calender" are some of the misspellings seen

Fitting In

regularly at businesses, restaurants and retail stores. "Rod" iron is one of my all-time favorites.

It's not a matter of being perfect, it's about being accurate. Reprint.

DRESS FOR SUCCESS ... NAH!

If it were up to me, I would go to work every day in my robe and bunny slippers.

And I would still crank out the finest news releases money could buy.

The fact that we evaluate people's creativity, skill and judgment by what they wear is shallow. And it only reinforces what an old departed colleague of mine once said: If you don't have an act, you better have a costume.

But for those of us who do have an act, why should we have to worry about our costume? When I first started out in corporate America in the mid '80s, if I hoped to get anywhere I had to wear skirted suits to work – not even pant suits. Nope, only secretaries and women who worked in the cafeteria would dare to wear pants. And these same women probably also wore low-cut blouses, flip-flops, dangling earrings and occasionally had a bra strap showing.

My, how times have changed.

Women now wear pants. Low-cut blouses aren't recommended but peeking bra straps are fashionable and flip-flops are made by designers. Go figure.

Dress codes keep evolving. Styles keep changing. Who would have believed that there

Fitting In

would ever be something called casual Friday and you could wear jeans to work?

Unfortunately, robes and bunny slippers haven't yet made the cut.

But I keep hoping.

Until then, just use common sense. Respect the need to dress appropriately for the job. If you have any doubts that an outfit will draw attention to yourself – and not in a good empowering way – then don't wear it. Otherwise, dress to feel good about yourself. Dress to like who you are. Dress to get the job done and be proud. Dress for *personal* satisfaction. It's the work that counts. Not the bunny slippers.

Pat Getter

WATCH YOUR LANGUAGE

I didn't need to hang around sailors or truck drivers to learn how to swear.

I can thank my mother for that.

And I assure you, the words that come from these lips would make even the most hardened longshoreman or Teamster blush badly.

But there's a time and place for letting those expletives fly out, and corporate America is neither.

Yes, there are still people with tender ears who are offended. You are best off just eliminating swear words from your vocabulary when you are at work. Yes, I know that isn't easy if you are used to speaking with peppery vocabulary as I am. But you also don't want to get a reputation for being crude.

Gauge the curse language tolerance by conversations with others over time. Hell and damn are probably OK. You might sneak in an s-word but better apologize for it and see what reaction you get. The f-word is still the hot potato and so I don't recommend dropping that bomb.

My first career was in television news. TV newsrooms are the antithesis of corporate America: As showtime approaches, they are very loud with obnoxious reporters blowing and going, definitely

Fitting In

swearing like sailors as they hustle to get their stories on the air.

Imagine being in television news for eight years and then making a transition to corporate America. That environmental change damn – oops – near killed me.

Fast forward 25 years later. I was back on TV working for a local county television station. About the second day I was there, the station manager was in an editing bay working with a videographer putting together a story. Something didn't go as he hoped and, exasperated, he said the f-word. Then, realizing I was standing behind him, he apologized. I laughed and told him I was actually *relieved* to hear him say it. Given that this was a local government TV facility, I was afraid it was going to be like corporate America. How wonderful to be back among real TV people where swearing is the norm! So really, not a fu@king problem!

JUNK YARD DOG, NOT PIT BULL

So, how do you navigate the pitfalls?

First, know your boundaries.

A senior executive at my Fortune-100 company took great pleasure in describing me as his junk yard dog. At first I wasn't sure if I should be happy or offended. But, after thinking a lot about it, I decided it was actually a compliment.

A junk yard dog is usually the reliable guy who keeps one eye half open even while taking a snooze. He knows the boundaries of his property and everything that is within it like the back of his paw. All who walk by are greeted by a disarming tail wag – just so long as they stay outside the fence line and keep moving. His name is probably Rufus or something like it and he appears to be friendly – but that's because you've never tried to enter the property without an invitation and so Rufus has never had to defend his property.

Our senior executive saw me in my public relations position much the same way as Rufus. I would deal with media in a friendly but not overly cozy way, knowing the boundaries of our metaphoric turf, but I stood ready at any given time to defend it – our corporate brand or image –

Fitting In

should the media make the challenge of trying to enter without an invitation.

But I was not some hoodlum's pit bull. I did not go after anyone or attack indiscriminately without obvious provocation.

So be a junk yard dog. Know the boundaries of your turf like the back of your paw. Greet everyone with a wag of your tail while you keep at least one eye on them at all times.

(I have nothing against pit bulls. First of all, there is no such breed as a pit bull. The term is used by people who don't know any better to describe three different breeds with similar characteristics. I know many sweet bullies or pitties, as they are affectionately known in the dog rescue community, who are excellent family pets. But, sadly, many pit bulls have been abused, usually by hoodlums, who turned into fighting dogs and have garnered a negative reputation, so it is in this context that I use the term.)

MAINTAIN INDIVIDUAL DIVERSITY

Second, maintain your individual diversity. Companies devote enormous resources to the issue of workplace diversity. Most focus on differences among races, gender, ethnicities, ages and those physically disabled.

There are other diversity issues worth noting that can be significant factors affecting performance when consistently ignored AND they matter to YOU.

Take, for example, co-workers who always start each day by standing in your office doorway asking did you have a good evening, what's new, telling you what TV show they watched last night or what they plan to do during lunch today. They might be amiable-amiable personalities who just feel they have to make pleasant conversation with colleagues to jump-start every work day. If you are a driver-driver personality, it probably makes you want to tear your hair out. Is that a workplace conflict of diversity? Absolutely-absolutely.

What about supervisors who consistently call for the weekly staff meeting to begin Monday at 8 a.m. The workday begins at 8 a.m. so that means if you want to get a cup of coffee, go to the bathroom – even take off your coat – you have to get to the office a little early. Apparently these supervisors are morning persons and always get to the office early anyway, so it's not a hardship for them to be ready to go by 8 a.m. – but it IS inconvenient for everyone else. Are these supervisors cognizant of the morning person/afternoon person conflict of diversity? No.

Speaking of getting a cup of coffee, many companies provide it free. Do you drink decaf? If coffee is being provided for free, is decaf also being provided for free? That's the regular/unleaded coffee diversity conflict.

But not everyone is a coffee drinker. Does the company also provide free tea and/or caffeine-free tea?

What about those folks who have to have their colas first thing in the morning? Which one: Coke or Pepsi? That debate alone can take hours; then you can tackle regular or diet, regular caffeine-free or diet caffeine-free.

These are all diversity issues. If company leaders want employees to believe that they care about what is important to them so that in the long term employees will be more productive, then company personnel need to listen. But they can't listen if you don't ask. So it starts with you. Don't be afraid to ask. Don't be afraid to maintain your individual diversity.

But keep in mind, the company doesn't have to provide any coffee, tea or soda for free. It may be that it can afford to order enough in bulk to keep the per-unit cost low but to order smaller quantities of many different products will raise their prices enough that they won't be able to justify the increased expense.

Sometimes you just can't look a gift horse in the mouth.

Be tolerant of the amiable-amiable who needs five minutes every morning of pleasantries to get started. I'm an amiable-expressive so I've been there. And if *you're* the amiable-amiable, think about how you might be imposing on the driver-driver.

The supervisor who calls a meeting at 8 straight up needs to be *gently* told that 8:15 a.m. would give *everyone else* a chance to take off their coats and hit the ground running. Get agreement on that first and maybe work toward changing to an after-lunch start time.

There are all levels of diversity we can accommodate if we just try-try.

Fitting In

Pat Getter

A SINGULAR SENSATION

And third, don't let anyone tell you or try to convince you that individual achievement is not important. If it weren't, they wouldn't name the most valuable player of the Super Bowl or the World Series. We wouldn't select best actors or actresses or motion pictures or television series each year. Individual achievement in business should be the same, and individuals should be encouraged to strive for individual recognition. Dale Earnhardt said it best: "Second place is just the first-place loser."

About the only time it's ever been important – the only time we've ever remembered anyone for coming in second or third in an event other than a horseracing trifecta – was when man stepped on the moon. But, after all, only **12 humans** have accomplished this feat – of a world population of about **7 billion**. OK, perhaps it is still worth noting all 12 of them. *(Can you name them? Answers below)*

Teamwork – specifically being a team player – is a good idea, but it demands great execution.

This business mantra has deteriorated into a process that ignores results, disdains leadership and promotes mediocrity. There may be a time and place for being a *team player* but why not just *play on a team*? One person cannot be a great quarterback and a wide receiver. One person cannot be a great pitcher and an outfielder. To be great at these positions requires unique skills. How many utility players make the Hall of Fame?

It takes a team effort to win the game and go on to a championship. But each individual player can shine in his position, be recognized for that achievement AND make an *individual* contribution to the *team* effort.

In corporate America, teamwork has too often come to mean consensus. Have to make a decision? Call a meeting and let the team decide. However, to reach consensus, aggressive, risky ideas often are rejected for moderate, safer ones. This brand of teamwork brings all team members down to the lowest common denominator so that consensus can be reached. But in the doing, consensus sometimes eliminates individuality, creativity and leadership. The results will be predictable, not extraordinary. If the decision is not successful, the responsibility is shared by everyone and therefore no individual is held liable. It also means there is no leadership.

When being a team player is the most important criteria for performance reviews and promotions, it is no wonder that employees hesitate to voice opinions outside of consensus. Those who do are quickly labeled as not being team players –

and these days that's the kiss of death, especially for anyone who already feels as though he does not fit in.

It's not enough to just play on a team. It needs to be a championship team. What we too often have now is akin to a boatful of rowers, each pulling in unison. One of the oarsmen cannot keep pace. But instead of replacing him, the others slow down to accommodate him. Now the team rows at a slower pace. Although the team always finishes the race, it never wins. A *team player* is expected to sacrifice his or her individual performance and achievement so that the team as a unit looks good. If you *play on a team,* the one who cannot keep pace is replaced with someone qualified to substitute so the rest of the team can compete at *its* level of ability.

My idea of teamwork is based on a baseball team. Each team player has been carefully chosen because he has the skills, experience and judgment necessary for his specific position. Each team player may shine in his own right, but no individual can play all positions and therefore cannot win a game by himself. It is still a *team effort.*

And so it should be in business. Always continue to work toward individual achievement. Never give up personal goals for success. Individual excellence inspires and supports the

Fitting In

team. Team excellence inspires and supports the individual.

(The 12 astronauts who walked on the moon are, in order: Neil Armstrong, Buzz Aldrin, Pete Conrad, Alan Bean, Alan Shepard, Ed Mitchell, Dave Scott, Jim Irwin, John Young, Charlie Duke, Gene Cernan and Jack Schmitt.)

ENJOY YOUR 15 MINUTES

If one day you discover you have achieved some fame or notoriety, please just embrace it.

The only thing worse than being recognized is NOT being recognized.

Not everyone will get the opportunity to be in the public spotlight, but if you do, enjoy it while it lasts.

When I was on television, people often came up to me and pointed out the obvious: you're that reporter on TV! I watch you all the time!

And anything else they mumbled in their exuberance was generally a repeat of what they already said: they recognize you, they watch you, they like you.

What's not to like about that?

Some who have achieved celebrity status – and my little bit of fame pales in comparison to what TV and movie stars get – argue that being stopped in restaurants and grocery stores intrudes into their personal lives.

I say there will come a day that you wished you were still recognized, so if you are lucky enough to get public recognition, enjoy it for all it's worth while you can.

Yes, it can be intrusive, but then again, you are out and around in public. My husband and I

Fitting In

were both on TV in Cincinnati and one evening while we were wheeling a cart through the supermarket, a man came up to us, pointed a finger and proclaimed, "it's you, isn't it!"

He then told us to "wait right there" and we could hear him yelling up and down the aisles looking for his wife so she could share the moment.

We agreed that we had no choice but to "wait right there" until he located his wife and then she, too, gushed about watching us all the time.

If it weren't such a sweet encounter, why would I remember it to this day with a smile?

But never be presumptuous. When people came up to me and said I looked familiar, I waited until they figured it out. How humiliating would it be if I said, "You probably saw me on television" and they responded, "No, I think it was at Walmart."

It doesn't take long to get snapped back into reality, so be gracious and be humble. If Andy Warhol's 1968 coined expression was accurate, then when you get your 15 minutes of fame, relish every second of it.

Pat Getter

DID YOU FIND IT?

At the end of a very long career or just a string of many unfulfilling jobs, will you be able to look at yourself and be satisfied that you still have your integrity and self-worth?

And if you are just starting a career or are somewhere in between, are you prepared for the challenges and pitfalls you may face?

You may be pummeled along the way but you will persevere and overcome the obstacles put before you if you believe in who you are and what you need to do to succeed when you feel like the square peg in the round hole of life:

I yam what I yam
Beggars can't be choosers
Emotional satisfaction won't last
We are all replaceable
Work for tomorrow
Take work seriously, not yourself
Two can keep a secret if one of them is dead
Keep your eye on the prize
Tell the emperor he's naked
Have a voice, earn a vote
Never assume anything
It's not wrong until it goes out wrong

Fitting In

If you don't have an act, you better have a costume
Dress for personal satisfaction
Watch your language
Be a junk yard dog
Maintain your individual diversity
Play on a baseball team
Enjoy your 15 minutes
Believe in yourself, be strong and laugh

You *will* be strong, not necessarily because you got everything you wanted, but because you never lost your self-respect.

And you still could laugh about it.

www.ingramcontent.com/pod-product-compliance
Lightning Source LLC
Chambersburg PA
CBHW061250040426
42444CB00010B/2338